D0178155

City Safari

Seagull

Isabel Thomas

Raintree

Raintree is an imprint of Capstone Global Library Limited, a company incorporated in England and Wales having its registered office at 7 Pilgrim Street, London, EC4V 6LB – Registered company number: 6695582

www.raintreepublishers.co.uk
myorders@raintreepublishers.co.uk

Text © Capstone Global Library Limited 2014
First published in hardback in 2014
The moral rights of the proprietor have been asserted.

Edited by Dan Nunn, Rebecca Rissman, and Helen Cox Cannons
Designed by Tim Bond
Original illustrations © Capstone Global Library Ltd 2014
Picture research by Mica Brancic
Production by Helen McCreath
Originated by Capstone Global Library Ltd
Printed and bound in China

ISBN 978 1 406 27129 4
17 16 15 14 13
10 9 8 7 6 5 4 3 2 1

British Library Cataloguing in Publication Data
A full catalogue record for this book is available from the British Library.

Acknowledgements
We would like to thank the following for permission to reproduce photographs: Alamy pp. 16 (© Stephen Dorey), 23 scavenge (© Nik Taylor Wildlife); Getty Images pp. 8 (Gordon Dixon), 10 (Jonathan Daniel), 11 (Taxi Japan/Hiroshi Watanabe), 17 (Photonica/Tony Cordoza), 23 loaf (Taxi Japan/Hiroshi Watanabe), 23 roost (Jonathan Daniel), Naturepl.com pp. 5 (2020VISION/© Peter Cairns), 6 (© David Tipling), 7 (2020VISION/© Terry Whittaker), 12 (© Graham Eaton), 13 (© Michael D. Kern), 14 (© Laurent Geslin), 19 (© David Tipling), 20 (© Ann & Steve Toon), 21 (© Markus Varesvuo), 23 flock (© Laurent Geslin); Rex Features pp. 18 and 23 mate (both Splashdown Direct); Shutterstock pp. 4 (© Marcin Wasilewski), 9 (© Elnur), 15 (© MelBrackstone), 23 roadkill (© Valeniker).

Front cover photograph of a seagull reproduced with permission of Shutterstock (© aaleksander). Back cover photograph of a seagull eating in a harbour reproduced with permission of Shutterstock (© Marcin Wasilewski).

We would like to thank Michael Bright for his invaluable help in the preparation of this book.

Every effort has been made to contact copyright holders of material reproduced in this book. Any omissions will be rectified in subsequent printings if notice is given to the publisher.

Warning!

Never touch wild animals or their homes. Some wild animals carry diseases. Scared animals may peck or scratch you, especially if they are protecting a nest. Never feed seagulls by hand, go near a seagull's nest, or touch seagull droppings.

Note about spotter icon

Your eyes, ears, and nose can tell you if a seagull if nearby. Look for these clues as you read the book, and find out more on page 22.

Contents

Some words are shown in bold, **like this**.
You can find them in the glossary on page 23.

Who has been spotted stealing food?

Grey and white feathers. Webbed feet. A hooked beak. It's a seagull!

You don't need to visit the seaside to see seagulls.

curved beak

black markings

red mark
on beak

They like to live in towns and cities, too.

Come on a city safari. Find out if seagulls
are living near you.

Why do seagulls live in towns and cities?

In the past, seagulls only lived near coasts.

There are fish and sea animals to eat, and cliffs to build nests.

Seagulls can find everything they need in towns and cities, too.

There are safe places to build nests. There is also food that humans leave behind.

What makes seagulls good at living in towns and cities?

Seagulls are very clever.

This makes them good at learning to live in new places.

Seagulls are bold and do not mind being close to people.

They can fly well and escape from danger quickly.

Where do seagulls rest?

Seagulls like to **roost** and **loaf** in groups.

Some choose high places such as roofs, away from dangers on the ground.

Others choose wide, open spaces, such as playing fields, car parks, and runways.

This means they can see danger coming.

What do seagulls eat?

Seagulls eat seeds, grains, and fruit, but they prefer meat.

They dive out of the sky to grab insects, worms, and fish.

Seagulls are good at **scavenging** for food.

They eat anything they find, such as bird eggs, **roadkill**, and even baby seagulls!

Why do seagulls like living near people?

Towns and cities are full of food that people throw away.

Flocks of seagulls fight over scraps in streets and parks.

Seagulls even steal food from people and pets.

They can help to keep cities clean by eating dead animals and litter.

What problems do seagulls cause in towns and cities?

Not everyone likes sharing a city with noisy seagulls.

Their droppings are messy. They can damage cars and buildings.

Seagulls that live near airports damage aeroplanes by flying into them.

People use spikes and nets to stop seagulls **roosting** or to scare them away.

Where do seagulls lay eggs?

Pairs of seagulls **mate** once a year.

They like to build nests in the same place every year.

They choose to nest in a different place from where they usually live and feed.

Both parents help to collect food and keep the eggs warm.

Why is it hard to spot baby seagulls?

Seagull chicks stay in the nest for several months.

Their parents chase any person or animal that gets too close.

When the young seagulls leave the nest, they are almost fully grown.

You can spot them by looking for patches of brown feathers.

Seagull spotter's guide

Look back at the sights, sounds, and smells that tell you a seagull might be nearby. Use these clues to go on your own city safari.

1 Seagulls learn where to find food, and keep coming back. They can make a mess by raiding bins and ripping open rubbish bags.

2 Seagulls make loud mewing and wailing calls. Large **flocks** can be very noisy.

3 Droppings show you where seagulls like to perch, **roost**, and nest.

4 If you see a seagull swooping down to attack someone, it is probably protecting a nest. Seagulls call loudly to scare people and animals away. If that doesn't work, they might peck and scratch.

Picture glossary

 **flock** group of birds eating, resting, or flying together

 **roadkill** dead animal that was killed crossing a road

 **loaf** rest or sit around without doing anything

 **roost** settle down to rest or sleep

 **mate** when a male and female animal get together to have babies

 **scavenging** looking for food that has been thrown away or left over

Find out more

Books

City Seagull, Dominic Bailey (Kindle Edition, 2012)

Wild Town, Mike Dilger (A & C Black, 2012)

Websites

www.bbc.co.uk/nature/life/Larus
Find out more about gulls on this BBC website.

http://www.rspb.org.uk/wildlife/birdguide/ families/gulls.aspx
The RSPB website has interesting information about gulls.

Index